Concrete Crafts

Making Modern Accessories
for the Home and Garden

ALAN WYCHECK

STACKPOLE
BOOKS

0 11557 03579 7

Copyright © 2010 by Stackpole Books

Published by
STACKPOLE BOOKS
5067 Ritter Road
Mechanicsburg, PA 17055
www.stackpolebooks.com

Printed in the United States of America

10 9 8 7 6 5

First edition

Cover design by Tessa Sweigert

Library of Congress Cataloging-in-Publication Data

Wycheck, Alan.
  Concrete crafts : making modern accessories for the home and garden / Alan
Wycheck. — 1st ed.
     p. cm.
  ISBN-13: 978-0-8117-3579-7
  ISBN-10: 0-8117-3579-6
  1. Handicraft. 2. House furnishings. 3. Garden ornaments and
furniture—Design and construction. 4. Concrete. I. Title.
  TT910.W93 2010
  745.5—dc22
                                                    2009022982

Contents

Introduction

This book will teach you how to make beautiful pavers, tiles, tables, bowls, and planters—all out of durable concrete. Unlike many craft books on the market, it is designed for anyone who likes to be creative and doesn't want to spend a lot of money on a new hobby. After reading the step-by-step instructions and completing the projects, you will have the necessary skills to make a variety of concrete crafts, including a concrete bowl that floats on water. All of the projects start with a simple design that you can build upon using your own creativity. It is best to read through each step of a project from start to finish before beginning that project. By doing so, you will have a good understanding of what will be required in the steps ahead, and each project will be a success.

Concrete touches our lives almost every day. We usually think of sidewalks and highways when we think of concrete; however, concrete can be beautiful as well as functional. It is the most-used man-made substance on our planet, with approximately 7 billion cubic yards used every year. To give you an idea of how much 7 billion cubic yards is, the Hoover Dam required 4.5 million cubic yards of concrete, which is enough to make a 4-foot-wide sidewalk around the entire world at the equator. And that's just one concrete project. Most concrete is used for architecture and civil engineering projects; estimates show that China uses about half of all the concrete in the world. The potential designs made with concrete are limited only by one's imagination. Although concrete is typically

Typical use of concrete.

heavy, even the issue of weight can be overcome when designing concrete products. This book is intended to introduce you to the world of concrete with practical, inexpensive projects that you can use for both function and art. These projects require basic tools that many of you probably already have, and if you don't have them, they are readily available. All of the projects can be made quickly and inexpensively. At the time of printing, a 94-pound bag of gray Portland cement costs about $10, and a premixed 80-pound bag costs about $5. I hope to instill in you the desire to further explore concrete crafting and come up with designs of your own.

Getting Started

Common sense is the rule when working with concrete. Use a dust mask and protective glasses when mixing concrete. Wet concrete is caustic and can cause skin irritation and burns. I tend to work with my bare hands, but if you are going to be in contact with wet concrete for long periods of time, you should definitely wear gloves. If you get concrete in your eyes, flush it out with clean water immediately. If you get it on your skin and it irritates you, wash it off with water. Cured concrete is nontoxic and as harmless as stone.

Making Concrete

Concrete is an amazing and versatile material that has been used for thousands of years. It can be made into almost any shape and size. The Egyptians used a primitive form of concrete to bond stone and brick. The Romans used it to make roadways and buildings. In our modern world, one would have a hard time making it through a day without walking on, driving over, or living with concrete. Concrete is made of three basic components: Portland cement, water, and aggregates (sand, gravel, rock, and so on). In standard concrete mixes, the amount of water

plays an important role in the hardness of the cured concrete. If too much water is added to a particular mix of concrete, it will be weaker than if the proper amount of water were added. The lightweight mixes we use in this book are not as hard or strong as the standard mixes, but they will work just fine in some projects.

The easiest way to make concrete is to purchase dry, premixed bags, which are available in home improvement stores, hardware stores, and concrete supply stores. Premixed bags range from 10 to 90 pounds, come in various name brands,

Common aggregate

On the left is $^1/_2$ inch or smaller limestone. On the right is pea gravel, the stone aggregate typically used in premixed bags of concrete. Notice the rounded shape of the pea gravel.

Some examples of lightweight aggregates. From left to right are perlite, peat moss, and vermiculite.

and are offered in several strengths. The strength is measured in pounds per square inch (psi); premixed bags range from about 2,500 psi to 6,000 psi. As mentioned earlier, the strength will be weakened if too much water is added to these dry mixes. I recommend high-strength concrete with fiber for the projects in this book. Concrete hardens to its full potential in about four weeks, at which time it can be measured for strength. The high-strength mixes I provide for you get very hard after twenty-eight days of curing.

The aggregate you choose plays a very important role in the concrete mix because it occupies the majority of the space. Aggregate is basically filler, but its different sizes, shapes, and composition affect the workability and strength of the concrete. You can typically add up to five parts aggregate; more than that will impede the concrete's workability. I recommend small limestone as an aggregate. Pea gravel, which is a rounded hard pebble, also works well, especially if it's exposed on the final project or used when making countertops with squared corners. The rounded form of the pea gravel allows the Portland cement and sand to thoroughly fill the corners of the mold. The sharp corners in the limestone aggregate can sometimes block the smaller aggregate—the sand—from filling the corners completely. Pea gravel, however, is not as strong as limestone. Also, acrylic fiber and water reducer are commonly added for additional strength. A standard concrete mix will yield about 3,500 psi.

Before starting, you need to determine the volume of concrete required for your project. An 80-pound bag of premixed concrete will make about 0.6 cubic feet of cured concrete. In other words, an 80-pound bag will provide a 24-inch square that is 2 inches thick. A list of helpful formulas to calculate volume is provided on page 154. Always make a little more concrete than you think you need. You can always fill a small mold, like a bowl or a tile, with any extra concrete.

Mixing Prepackaged Concrete

1. Place the bag of dry concrete mix in a wheelbarrow or mixing trough.

2. Cut open the bag.

3. Dump the entire contents of the bag into the wheelbarrow.

4. Add about ³/₄ gallon of water to the dry mix a little at a time.

5. Use a shovel to thoroughly work the water into the dry mix.

6. Add more of the water and work it in.

7. Work all of the water into the dry mix.

8. Scrape to the bottom of the mix, and when you think it is mixed thoroughly, mix a little more.

9. Work the concrete until there is no dry mix visible. It should resemble this photo when it's ready to be used.

Concrete Recipes

Standard Concrete Mix

1 part Portland cement
2 parts sand
3 parts stone
(Fiber mesh and water reducer may also be added
for increased strength)

Craft Concrete Mix

This mix is more workable than the standard mix.
It creates a claylike concrete.
1 part Portland cement
2 parts sand
2 parts aggregate
1 handful of acrylic fiber (optional)
2 ounces of water reducer (not readily available, but
if you can find it, use it)

Lightweight Concrete Mix

Bowls made from this mix will actually float on water,
though it's not as strong as the other mixes. The
lightweight concrete mix can be used for any of the
projects in this book with the exception of the tiles
and pavers, which have to support foot traffic. Also
known as hypertufa, this is a modern formula that
holds up well in any weather. For instructions on
making a hypertufa planter, see pages 115–117.
$1^1/_2$ parts Portland cement
2 parts horticultural perlite
2 parts sphagnum peat moss
1 pinch of fiber mesh
$^1/_2$ cup of acrylic bonding agent (optional)
2 ounces of water reducer (optional)
Enough water to make a claylike mixture

Concrete recipes are measured in parts, or units. In
other words, one part equals one bucket, one
scoop, or one of whatever measuring device you're
using. By using a 16-ounce cup as your unit (one
part), you will have enough concrete to make a small
bowl or planter about 12 inches in diameter, 7 inches
tall, and 1 inch thick. A 5-gallon bucket (one part) will
yield enough concrete to make the 22-inch tapered
planter in chapter 6 with some left over. The standard
concrete recipe will contain six parts of material: one
of Portland cement, two of sand, and three of stone.
Portland cement acts as the glue that holds all of the
ingredients together.

Portland cement is typically sold in 94-pound
bags that contain 1 cubic foot of material. The only
difference between gray and white Portland cement
is the color, which results from the oxides used in the
manufacturing process. White Portland cement is
manufactured with raw materials that contain less
iron oxide and magnesium oxide, the ingredients
that give gray Portland cement its color. White Portland cement is generally used to produce either bril-
liant whites or vibrant colors; the latter is achieved by
using color additives. Portland cement is made from
a mix of calcium carbonate (limestone), alumina, sil-

ica, and iron oxide. It is available in eight different
types; for most common applications, Type I is used.
The other types are for a variety of specific uses.

You can add up to five parts of aggregate without affecting the concrete's strength. This will
depend on the strength of the aggregate, however.
For instance, limestone is much stronger than perlite.
More aggregate will also affect the concrete's workability. I recommend small limestone as a standard
aggregate. Pea gravel also works well, especially if it's
exposed on the final project, but it's not as strong as
limestone. You may eventually want to experiment
with different mixes and aggregates. Acrylic fiber and
water reducer are commonly added for additional
strength. The standard concrete mix will yield about
3,500 psi.

Mixing the Concrete Recipes

We will use the concrete craft recipe for this example and mix it in a small electric mixer. A wheelbarrow or mixing trough can be used instead of the electric mixer. Regardless of the mixing container that you use, choose a measuring device for the parts that will allow adequate room for mixing after all the ingredients are in your mixing container. If you use a wheelbarrow or trough, add the ingredients in the order as described in the electric mixer example, then blend them with a shovel as described in the pre-mixed concrete example on pages 4–6.

Note: Always wear a dust mask when mixing concrete!

1. Load the mixer with two buckets (parts) of limestone.

2. Turn on the mixer and saturate the stone with water.

3. Add about 2 ounces of water reducer (optional).

Your mix should look like this. Notice the foam created by the water, water reducer, and lime dust from the stone.

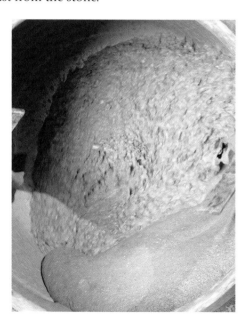

Note: Water reducers are commonly used in today's concrete mixes. They produce a chemical reaction during the hydration process that makes the mixture more liquid with minimal water. They range in strength and can reduce the amount of water used in a mix up to 40 percent, thereby increasing the strength of the concrete. The water reducer in this mix causes the concrete to feel more like clay.

4. Slowly add one bucket (part) of Portland cement and let the mixer run for a few minutes until the cement is evenly distributed through the aggregate.

The Portland cement will cling to the stone.

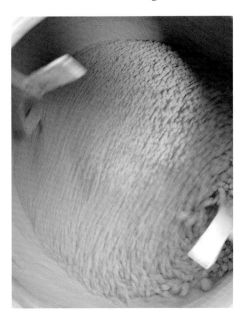

Note: I recommend adding the Portland cement to the stone because the Portland cement often clumps in the bag from moisture and compression. The moving stone tends to break up these clumps.

5. Add more water.

At this point, the mix should look like sticky, wet clay.

6. Add a small handful of fiber to the mix.

7. Sprinkle the fiber into the mix a little at a time so it mixes throughout the concrete evenly.

8. Slowly add two buckets (parts) of sand.

The mix should look a little dry.

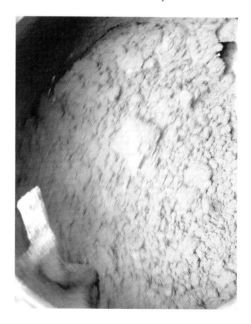

9. Add small amounts of water at a time. Remember, your concrete will be weakened if you add too much water to your mix.

The concrete should look like sticky oatmeal and peel off the sides of the mixer as it spins.

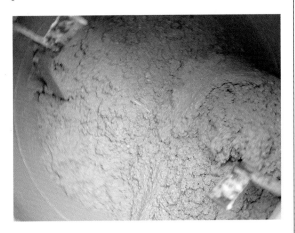

10. **Optional:** Add color to the mix. Allow it to mix thoroughly.

I have always had success mixing concrete using this method. Concrete recipes often call for exact amounts of water, but I have found that if you keep your mix on the dry side throughout the process, you will produce workable concrete that cures strong and hard. Be patient when you are mixing and allow the water to thoroughly mix with all of the elements in the batch. Some of the projects in this book will work better with a more liquid mixture of concrete. It is best to make concrete more liquid with the use of water reducer.

Projects

1. Pavers

Supplies

- ³/₄-inch plywood
- 3-inch x 1-inch x 8-foot boards
- 1³/₄-inch coarse drywall screws
- Concrete mold release (vegetable oil or motor oil work well)
- Fiberglass resin
- Paint roller or brush
- 100 percent silicone caulk

Making a Square Mold

The first step in shaping concrete is to make a mold into which the concrete will be poured. The following steps will teach you how to make a simple 2-foot-square mold that will render a finished paver 2 feet square by 1³/₄ inch thick. Like most of the projects in this book, your finished dimensions may vary slightly due to shrinkage, slight miscalculations, and other variables. You will find that the irregularities in all of the projects in this book are what make them beautiful and unique.

Note: The 8-foot length and 4-foot width of a sheet of plywood are fairly accurate. But the thickness is not what you may expect. In the United States, plywood is actually measured in $1/32$-inch increments. Therefore, a sheet that is labeled $3/4$ inch is actually $23/32$ inch. Similarly, a $1/2$-inch sheet is $15/32$ inch and a $1/4$-inch sheet is $7/32$ inch. Also, board thicknesses are not exact measurements as shown on the label. A board labeled 3" x 1" x 8' is actually $2^1/2$" x $3/4$" x 8'. A good chart that shows the actual dimensions of finished wood can be found at www.woodbin.com.

1. Decide how many pavers you want and the amount of wood you will need. If you want to pave a large area, make several molds at one time.

2. Select good quality $3/4$-inch-thick plywood and straight 3-inch x 1-inch x 8-foot boards. I like to use $3/4$-inch-thick plywood because of its durability and rigidity.

3. Get a 2 x 2–foot square of plywood.

Note: Many building supply stores sell precut 2 x 2–foot plywood pieces. They also usually have a panel cutter in-house and will cut plywood for you in any size for free. But if you want to cut it for yourself, follow these steps:

1. Make sure the edges of the plywood are square, then mark 24 inches on the long side of the plywood.

2. Mark 24 inches on the short dimension of the plywood.

3. Cut out the square.

Note: If you are going to make several molds at one time, cut a 24-inch x 8-foot piece of plywood.

1. Mark 24 inches on the short dimensions of your plywood.

2. Cut the plywood along the length after marking a 24-inch reference line.

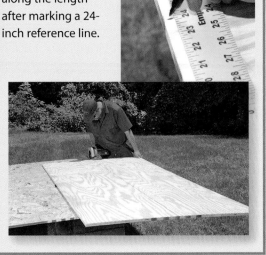

Constructing the Mold

All the surfaces of the mold that will be in contact with the concrete should be coated with fiberglass resin. I use Bondo brand, which is available in most auto parts stores. Concrete will stick to wooden surfaces even if a release agent is used. While you don't have to use fiberglass resin, if you do, your molds will last longer and, most importantly, your concrete will slip out easily.

1. Prepare the wooden surface for the fiberglass resin by brushing off any sawdust.

2. Prepare a small quantity of fiberglass resin. Carefully follow the manufacturer's instructions. Use small amounts of resin at a time because it only has about a 10-minute working time.

3. Add hardener.

4. Mix thoroughly.

5. Pour the mixed resin onto the plywood.

6. Spread the resin evenly over one side of the plywood with a smooth-surface paint roller.

7. Make sure every bit of the wood is covered.

8. Coat one side of the 3 x 1–inch boards at the same time you are coating the plywood with fiberglass resin.

9. Allow the fiberglass resin to harden, then apply a second coat.

10. Take notice of any low spots on the wood and try to make the surface as even as possible.

11. To make the mold's side pieces, mark two resin-coated 3 x 1–inch boards at 24 inches (after the resin has dried).

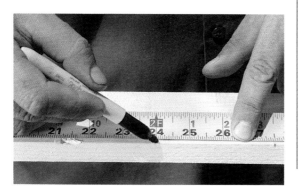

12. Cut the boards.

Note: We are using a miter saw to ensure our cut is square. A circular saw or a hand saw, however, will work just fine.

13. Mark two resin-coated 3 x 1–inch boards at 25$\frac{1}{2}$ inches.

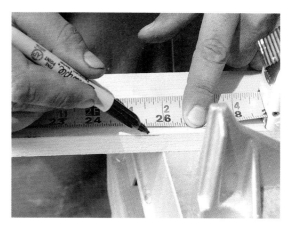

14. You can cut two boards at a time to ensure better consistency. Make sure the ends are perfectly flush.

15. Mark the resin-coated plywood at 24 inches.

16. Cut the plywood along the 24-inch line.

17. Attach the 24-inch, resin-coated, 3 x 1-inch board to the side of the resin-coated plywood.

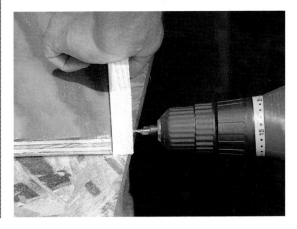

18. Make sure the resin-coated sides are on the inside of the mold. Predrill a hole with a countersink bit.

19. Attach the pieces by inserting a 1³/₄-inch coarse drywall screw.

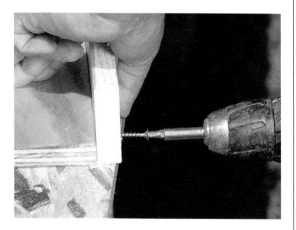

20. Continue attaching the rest of the 24-inch side in the same manner by predrilling and screwing 1³/₄-inch screws 3 to 4 inches apart.

21. Attach the 25¹/₂-inch side in the same fashion.

Note: It is best to predrill and countersink the screws so you don't split the wood. Predrilling also helps draw the two pieces of wood tighter together.

The corners should look like this.

The finished mold should look like this. Note that the resin-coated surfaces are all facing inward.

22. Apply 100-percent silicone caulk to all the inside corners of the mold.

23. Smooth the caulk with your finger.

24. Wrap a strip of duct tape around the outside of the mold to cover all the screw heads.

Note: It is recommended to cover the screw heads with tape in case the mold has to be disassembled to remove the cured concrete. If concrete gets into the screw heads, it makes it very difficult to take out the screws.

Pouring, Curing, and Releasing Concrete from the Mold

Now that you know how to make the concrete and a square mold, it is time to make a paver.

1. Spray a release agent onto all surfaces that will be in contact with the concrete.

Note: A release agent is any type of substance that helps prevent the concrete from bonding to the mold. There are products formulated specifically for concrete mold release, but the cheapest vegetable oil or motor oil will work just as well.

2. Make sure the mold is positioned so you can access the underside. Then pour some concrete into the mold.

3. Vibrate the underside of the mold with a palm sander or a concrete vibration tool.

4. Vibrate on all sides of the form. The concrete will quickly settle until it is level.

Note: If you don't have a vibrating tool, tap the mold hard on all sides or lift it up slightly and slam it down. The concrete will level out.

5. Add more concrete and continue to vibrate.

6. Add exactly enough concrete so that the top surface of the concrete is flush with the top surface of the mold. If you add too much, just screed off the excess with a straight board, as shown below.

7. Thoroughly vibrate your paver until it looks like this.

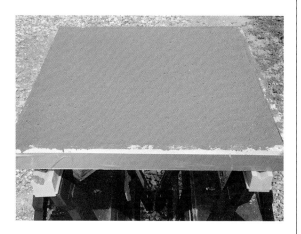

8. Cover the concrete and allow it to cure in the mold for at least 24 hours at 70 degrees F or warmer before removing it from the mold. Allow for a longer curing time in colder weather.

Note: Concrete doesn't dry, it cures. Curing times vary depending on humidity, temperature, and water content of the concrete. Don't pour concrete when the temperature is below 40 degrees F. Most of the projects in this book require only a 24-hour curing period at 70 degrees F or warmer before they can be removed from the mold. The bowl projects with thin sides, however, should cure for at least 48 hours because they are very delicate. The lightweight concrete mixes should be left to cure in the mold for at least three days. The longer the concrete stays covered in the mold, the stronger it will be. Concrete will reach nearly 100 percent of its strength in 28 days. Concrete also tends to shrink slightly as it cures, making it easier to remove from the mold.

9. Remove the concrete paver from the mold. Notice how flat the top surface of the paver is—it took the exact shape of the bottom of the mold. This is the same technique used in making countertops and tabletops. You can also trowel the top surface of flat concrete, but it will never come out perfectly flat as it does when poured onto a perfectly flat mold.

Making Colored and Textured Pavers

Now that you understand the basics of concrete and mold-making, we will move on to some variations. After all, you could just go to your local home improvement store and buy gray concrete pavers, but with your newly gained knowledge, you can make pavers of various sizes, textures, and colors.

1. Textured and colored pavers are easy to make. First, coat the mold with a release agent.

2. Sprinkle a few handfuls of sand onto the bottom of the mold.

3. Sprinkle some color of your choice onto the bottom of the mold. A little color goes a long way.

> **Note:** Concrete color additives are made from oxidized metals and come in powdered, granular, or liquid form. There are many different brands available that can be found in home improvement and concrete supply stores.

4. Fill the mold with concrete.

5. Push the concrete into the mold with a straight board or trowel and screed off the excess.

> **Note:** Do not vibrate the mold for this technique. If you vibrate, the sand will mix with the concrete and you will lose the sandy texture that we are trying to achieve.

6. After the concrete cures and is removed from the mold, wash off the excess sand and color.

Notice the interesting textures and colors this technique renders.

You may want to stain the surface of your pavers. Staining is discussed in detail on page 47. If you want only texture and no color, the result will look like this.

Another variation is to sprinkle black sand onto the mold to produce veins of black on the pavers.

Note: Besides working well as a mold release agent, used motor oil will produce concrete with a nice gray color on the surfaces that touched it. The concrete holds the solids from the used oil, creating a nice patina.

Again, if you want texture, do not vibrate the concrete once it's placed in the mold. Vibrating will cause the black sand to mix with the wet concrete. Use a screed or trowel to press the concrete into the mold.

Each paver will have its own unique pattern that will help create an interesting look when grouped with other pavers.

2. Tiles

Tiles are essentially thin pavers. This project will teach you how to make a tray with eight cells that will render eight 18 x 18 x ³/₄-inch tiles and two cells that will render two 18 x 15 x ³/₄-inch tiles. This practical setup is useful if you want to tile a small entryway or bathroom floor. If you want to make a lot of tiles, construct several trays. When you are comfortable with the techniques, experiment with different shapes and colors on your own. If you want tiles sized differently than this example, simply adjust the cuts to fit your desired dimensions.

1. Following the manufacturer's instructions, mix small amounts of fiberglass resin at a time by adding the suggested amount of hardener to the resin. The workability time for fiberglass resin is only about 10 minutes, so it's best to not make large batches at once.

You can use a clean scrap of wood to gently stir the mixture.

2. Cover the entire surface of the plywood with fiberglass resin. Remember that the concrete will take on the exact texture of the surface that it is poured on. Coating with resin is optional, but it will enable you to reuse your tray many times and produce a smooth textured tile.

Foam brushes also work well for applying the resin.

3. Although not necessary, sanding the resin after it dries will create a super-smooth surface. Reapply another coat of fiberglass resin if necessary.

4. Level the surface you are going to work on.

5. Place the plywood squarely on your working surface with the resin-coated surface facing up.

6. Cut twelve 18-inch sections from the 1-inch x 2-inch x 8-foot boards.

7. Attach a 1-inch x 2-inch x 8-foot board squarely along a long edge of the plywood, as shown.

8. Attach a 1 x 2 x 18–inch board perpendicular and squarely to the end of the 8-foot board.

9. Position another 8-foot section of board exactly 18 inches parallel to the 8-foot board that is already secured to the plywood. Place an 18-inch board along the bottom, along the left side, and along the top within the three-sided framework, as shown.

10. Secure the 8-foot board near the intersection of the 18-inch section.

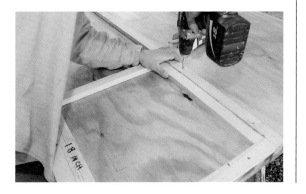

11. Push the 18-inch section that's opposite the attached piece tight against the top and bottom 18-inch guides and secure it to the plywood.

You'll have a near-perfect 18-inch square cell after you remove the two unattached guide pieces.

12. Move the guides to the other side of the left-hand piece, and add another 18-inch piece to the side to create the next cell of the tray.

13. Continue making the cells in the same manner. Make sure the boards butt squarely against one another.

14. Make a second row of cells the same as the first row.

If you've cut the 18-inch boards accurately, the cells should come together squarely.

15. Make sure all of the cells are square by butting all of the boards tight together before securing them to the plywood. Continue to the end.

16. The last two cells will be about 3 inches shorter than the rest. The tiles from the last two cells will be about 18 x 15 inches and can be used as cut pieces when the tiles are installed.

You could do all of the screwing by hand, but a drill or electric screwdriver will make things go much quicker.

17. Optional: It is not necessary to caulk the corners of the cells, but if you want rounded tile edges, you should now caulk them with a thin bead of 100-percent silicone caulk.

18. Cover all of the screw heads with small pieces of tape. It's important to cover the screw heads in this project because many of the screws may have to be removed in order to release the cured concrete.

19. Coat the insides of the cells with a release agent.

Use a rag to wipe release agent onto every interior surface including the sides. Reapply agent as needed.

The tray is now ready to be filled with concrete.

20. Place some concrete in a few cells.

21. Push the concrete around with a trowel so it sits evenly in each cell. Fill all the cells.

22. Vibrate every area you can access, including the underside of the tray.

23. Use a trowel and vibrator together to level any uneven spots.

24. Continue vibrating until the concrete is level.

25. Cover the concrete and allow it to cure one to two days, depending on the temperature.

26. After the concrete has cured sufficiently, remove the tape that covers the screws.

27. Remove the screws.

28. Remove the boards. Sometimes the tiles will slip out easily, so try to remove as few boards as possible. This will make it easier to reassemble the mold later.

29. Slip a putty knife under each tile, being careful not to scratch them. *Do not pry up the tiles from the corner because that is the weakest point.* They should lift easily off the resin-coated plywood. Remember, the tiles are not fully cured. Concrete at this state of curing is referred to as "green."

30. Remove the rest of the tiles.

Work carefully. The tiles can chip or crack if handled roughly.

Notice the moisture in the tiles at this stage. This moisture will eventually evaporate.

"Bug holes," or "honeycombs," are trapped air pockets caused from insufficient vibrating. They can be filled in with Portland cement or unsanded grout if you wish. Instructions for how to fill in bug holes can be found on page 44.

Note: Imperfections are what make these projects interesting. None of the projects in this book will look mass-produced or machine-made. Corners that are not exactly square or sizes that are inconsistent will be noticeable when the tiles are installed, but that's not necessarily a bad thing. Everybody will have their own comfort level with imperfections. To me, some of the most interesting things—as well as people—are far from perfect.

Making a Smooth-Surfaced Tile Tray

This tray is constructed much like the previous example with a few exceptions. The result will be an extremely smooth-surfaced tile.

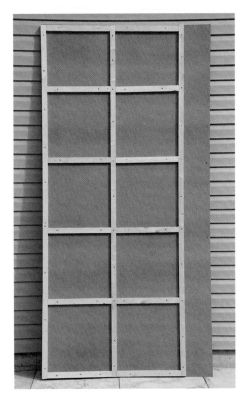

Supplies

One sheet $1/8$ x 48 x 96–inch hardboard
One sheet $5/8$ x 48 x 96–inch particleboard
Six 1 x 2 x 96–inch boards
Mold release agent

1. Lay a $1/8$ x 48 x 96–inch piece of hardboard on top of a $5/8$ x 48 x 96–inch piece of particleboard. (The hardboard sheet is too thin to use without the particleboard backing.)

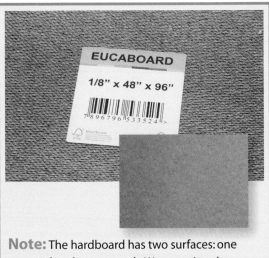

Note: The hardboard has two surfaces: one textured and one smooth. We are using the smooth side.

2. Align the corners of the particleboard and hardboard, then build 18-inch square cells as shown in the previous example.

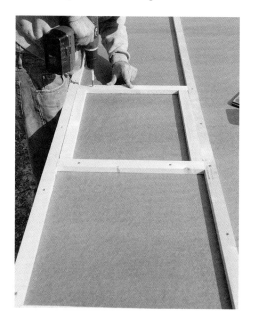

3. Continue building one cell at a time until you reach the end.

4. Coat the inside of the cells with a mold release.

Note: Do not paint the hardboard with fiber-glass resin because it won't be as smooth as the oiled hardboard surface.

5. Fill and vibrate the cells as in the previous example. Vibrate as much air out of the concrete as possible.

6. Smooth the exposed surface.

The advantage of this tray is that it renders very smooth-surfaced tiles and is very inexpensive (a sheet of hardboard costs less than $10). The disadvantage is that you can only get one or two pours per sheet of hardboard.

Filling "Bug Holes"

1. Place the tile on a flat and level surface. You can finish many tiles at the same time if you prefer.

2. Look for bug holes and imperfections that you want to fill in with Portland cement or unsanded grout.

Note: Everyone has their own definition of perfection. This tile was chosen to illustrate how to fill in "bug holes" because of the excessive amount of them; this is not a typical tile. Bug holes are formed from trapped air and usually indicate inadequate vibration during the pouring stage. It's not absolutely necessary to fill in the holes because the sealer will settle into them when it's applied later.

3. Mix a small amount of Portland cement or unsanded grout and water together and stir.

4. The mixture should be smooth and liquid.

5. If you are working on a small area, work the mixture into the holes with a putty knife.

6. If you have a larger area to fill, work the mixture into the holes with a trowel.

7. Continue working the cement into the holes and scraping off the excess cement until the holes are filled.

8. Allow the cement to dry, then sand off the excess. It's not necessary to allow the cement to cure 100 percent before you sand it.

9. Brush off all of the cement dust.

10. Wipe the tile clean with a damp sponge or rag. Go from one end to the other in a single direction. A back-and-forth motion doesn't pull the dirt off, it rubs it in.

> **Note:** You can apply more cement and repeat this process to get a smoother surface if you choose.

Finishing the Concrete Tiles

Now that you have gray concrete tiles, you can color them in countless ways. I chose to illustrate a simple method that produces a beautiful and durable finish. I recommend using Smith's Color Floor stains, made especially for concrete. They are very easy to work with and are extremely durable.

Applying Stain

1. Choose stains you think will complement each other. We chose Sandstone for the background color with Mars Red, Dark Chocolate, and Nutmeg for the complementary colors.

2. Pour distilled water into a spray bottle.

3. Squeeze the stain concentrate into the water. Refer to the manufacturer's mixing instructions.

4. Spray the entire tile with the background color.

6. Drip one of the three complementary colors onto the background color with a small foam brush. Notice how it mixes with the background.

5. Mix the other three colors.

7. Drip the other colors onto the tile. You can flick the brush to create interesting splatters, or simply let the stain drip. There really is no wrong way to apply the stain.

8. The colors will all blend together to form an interesting pattern of color.

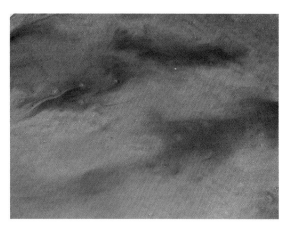

9. The stain will lighten considerably as it dries.

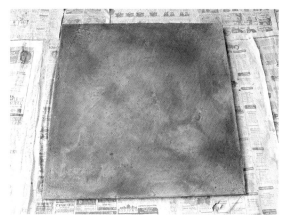

Notice all of the interesting colors and textures.

10. Seal the tile with a durable sealer. Apply the sealer with a foam brush or a spray bottle. The blue of this sealer will disappear and dry clear.

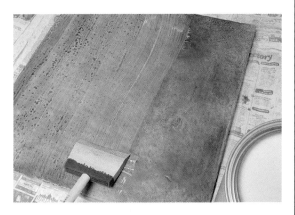

11. Allow the tile to dry and cure thoroughly before installing it.

3. Round Tabletop

This is one of my favorite projects in the book. The $1\frac{1}{2}$-inch-deep, 24-inch-round patio side tabletop is simple, practical, and durable, and no one in your neighborhood will have one. Like all of the projects, you will first need to construct a mold to form the concrete. Once you learn how to make a round mold, you will also be able to make the stepping stones described in chapter 5.

Supplies

- Two 24-inch square pieces of plywood at least $\frac{3}{4}$ inch thick
- One $2\frac{1}{2}$ x 80–inch long strip of hardboard
- $1\frac{1}{4}$-inch drywall screws
- One 80-pound bag of premixed concrete
- One tube of acrylic caulk

Making a Round Mold

1. Select a good quality piece of ⅝-inch or ¾-inch plywood and cut a 2-foot square from it. You will have to cut a 24-inch diameter circle from the square. The following steps illustrate a simple method for marking the circle.

2. Find the center of the square by measuring diagonally from one corner to the opposite corner and marking the center point. Then do the same for the other two corners. Where the marks intersect is the center of the plywood.

3. Cut a 1 x 2–board about 16 inches long. This scrap board will be used to mark a circle.

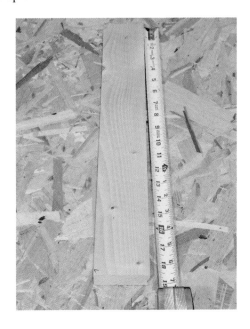

4. Mark at 2 inches and 14 inches from one end of the board.

5. Drill a $^1/_8$-inch hole at the 2-inch mark and a $^1/_2$-inch hole at the 14-inch mark. The $^1/_2$-inch hole should be big enough to fit a Sharpie or other marker through.

6. Push a drywall screw that is at least $1^1/_2$ inches through the small hole and align the tip with the middle of the mark on the plywood.

7. Tighten the screw to the plywood so it draws the board and plywood together, but not so tight that you can't move the board.

8. Insert a marker and draw a circle onto the plywood.

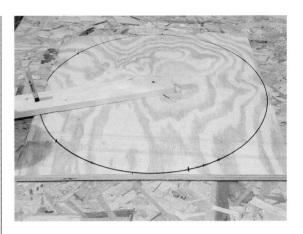

9. Remove the screw and the board. If you've measured carefully, you will have made a perfect 24-inch diameter circle.

10. Cut out the circle using a jigsaw. This piece of plywood will be used for the mold.

11. Mark another piece of plywood with a 20-inch circle using the same technique as before (but measuring and drilling only a 10-inch span on the scrap piece). This piece will be used to mount the tabletop onto its base.

12. Cut out the 20-inch circle.

You should have two circles that look like this.

13. The next step is to make the sides of the mold. Mark out a strip of hardboard $2^{1}/_{2}$ inches wide by 76 inches long.

14. Cut the strip.

15. Soak the strip with water to make it pliable enough to wrap around the outside of the 24-inch wood circle.

16. Secure one end of the strip to the plywood with a 1¼-inch drywall screw, as shown. Make sure the bottom of the strip is flush with the bottom of the plywood circle.

17. Bend the strip around the larger plywood circle.

18. Attach the strip to the plywood by securing it with screws every few inches.

19. Mark where the strip overlaps.

20. Cut at the overlap mark.

21. Attach the end of the strip.

22. Cut another short strip of hardboard about 12 inches long to support the seam.

23. Attach the support strip.

Your mold should look like this.

24. Apply acrylic caulk and smooth over the seam so it won't leave a line on the edge of the tabletop.

25. Apply a heavy bead of acrylic caulk around the inside corner of the mold.

Note: Use a small bead of acrylic caulk if you do not want a large radius on the edge of your circular tabletop. Remember, the bottom of the mold will be the top of the table. Acrylic caulk is used in this project because it will be covered with fiberglass resin after it cures. In projects where the caulk will make direct contact with the concrete, 100-percent silicone caulk is used because silicon doesn't stick to concrete.

26. Use a 1-inch diameter pipe or dowel to create a smooth 1-inch radius. The idea is to create an angle of caulk so the finished tabletop won't have a sharp edge.

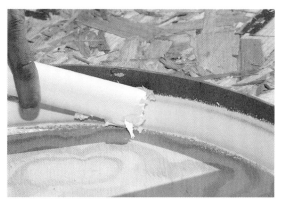

27. Wet your finger and smooth out the high spots.

28. Apply a few coats of fiberglass resin after the caulk thoroughly cures (see the label for the recommended curing time). Sand in between coats.

29. The 20-inch mounting circle will be embedded in the bottom of the tabletop to allow the piece to be attached to a base. Apply several coats of resin to the 20-inch circle. It's important that the circle is covered thick with resin because if water gets into it when it is in the cured concrete, it may expand and crack the tabletop. As an alternative, you can saturate the mounting circle with oil instead of covering it with fiberglass resin.

30. Screw 1¼-inch drywall screws around the circumference of the mounting circle every few inches, leaving a ¼ inch or so exposed. This will ensure the mounting circle does not move in the finished tabletop. This step is optional. If the mounting circle ever loosens from the concrete, just glue it into place with construction glue. The small screws, however, will prevent it from moving at all.

31. Mount two 4-inch blocks of wood on the mold directly across from each other. Make sure the blocks of wood are shorter than the mold. These blocks will support the mounting circle.

32. The mounting circle will be suspended above the mold on a 28-inch crossbar board to allow it to be embedded in the underside of the tabletop. Center and attach a 28-inch board directly across the middle of the mounting circle, then attach the crossbar board to the blocks, as shown.

33. Make sure the mounting circle is centered on the mold. There should be a 2-inch gap all the way around the perimeter.

34. Now remove one end of the crossbar board from one of the blocks. This will allow you to add the concrete. It's important to be able to reattach the mounting circle in the same centered position after some concrete is poured into the mold—make sure to reuse the same screw hole.

Pouring Concrete into the Mold

1. Coat the inside of the mold with a mold release agent.

2. If you want color in your tabletop, sprinkle it into the mold now. The color will mix with the concrete and create a marbled effect.

3. Fill the mold halfway with concrete.

4. Reattach the mounting circle.

5. Vibrate the sides and underside of the mold thoroughly. A palm sander makes a great concrete vibrator.

6. Carefully fill the mold the rest of the way.

7. Fill and vibrate the mold until the concrete levels at the top.

8. After the concrete cures, remove the brace that holds the mounting circle.

9. Remove the cured concrete from the mold. It should slip out easily because of the 1-inch radius, resin coating, and mold release. If it doesn't, remove a few screws from the mold.

10. Wash off excess color.

Creating a Sandy Texture with Acid

For a sandstone texture, you can spray the cured concrete with diluted muriatic acid, which can be found in home improvement and hardware stores. The more diluted the acid, the less reaction it will create. A 1:20 solution is a good starting point. You should always wear protective gloves and glasses when working with acid.

1. Following the manufacturer's directions, mix the acid into the water, not the water into the acid. One part acid to twenty parts water is a good ratio.

2. Spray the acid onto the concrete and watch it react. Keep fresh water on hand to stop the chemical reaction.

3. The acid will react violently with the metal oxide from the colorant.

4. Repeat spraying with acid and fresh water until you achieve your desired effect.

5. The concrete will get a worn look.

6. After you are done with the acid wash, thoroughly wash out the sprayer with water.

The acid will destroy the internal mechanism of the sprayer if it isn't cleaned out.

7. Smooth off any rough edges with a brick rub.

8. Sand any concrete off the mounting circle.

9. Get creative with your table base. Here we used a pedestal table base that was being thrown away from a local restaurant. We replaced the center post with a locust tree root.

10. Once you decide on a table base, check to see if you like the color combination.

11. If you want to stain the concrete with additional colors, do so at this time.

Note: There are dozens of different concrete sealers available. A nongloss oil base sealer was used for this piece.

12. Once you are happy with the colors, seal the concrete.

13. Finally, mount the concrete tabletop to the base. Use galvanized screws, which won't rust.

This beautiful, unique table will add a creative touch to your outdoor décor.

Heavy driftwood also makes a great base. You could also search for an antique table and replace the top with a handmade concrete one.

4. Game Table

Supplies

- One 24-inch square piece of plywood at least $1/2$ inch thick
- Two 13 x 6–inch pieces of plywood $5/8$ inch thick
- Two 1 x 2 x 20–inch boards
- Two 1 x 2 x 21$1/2$–inch boards
- Two 1 x 2 x 22–inch boards
- Thirty-two dark-colored 1$3/4$-inch glass tiles
- Thirty-two light-colored 1$3/4$-inch glass tiles
- One 20-inch square piece of clear contact paper
- 1$1/4$-inch coarse drywall screws
- 2-inch coarse drywall screws
- white typing paper

This project builds on what you've already learned; the game table is essentially a paver with glass inlays. You can use the inlay technique to make more complex mosaics of your own design. For simplicity's sake, however, we will make a chessboard with symmetric squares.

1. Select a level working surface for your project.

2. Cut or purchase a 24-inch square piece plywood at least $1/2$ inch thick. Identify the squarest corner—all measurements will start at this corner.

3. Cover the board with white typing paper. Guidelines drawn onto this paper will act as a pattern for placing the glass squares.

4. Mark the center of the paper-covered plywood by measuring off of the corner identified in step 2.

5. Draw a line through the center mark.

6. Mark the center of the line you just drew.

7. Draw a line through the center mark perpendicular to the line on the paper.

8. Draw a 20-inch square box centered on the guidelines (2 inches in from all four edges of the wood).

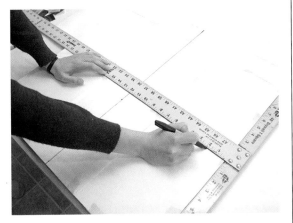

You will now have center guidelines and the outside perimeter of the table.

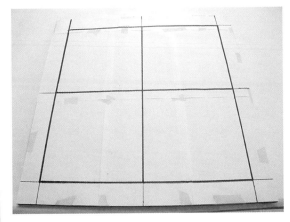

9. Separate the two layers of contact paper.

10. Tape the contact paper *sticky side up* to the pattern, attaching only the edges of the contact paper to the pattern.

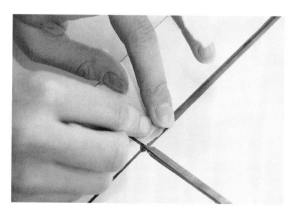

The contact paper should be secured to the pattern as illustrated in the photo.

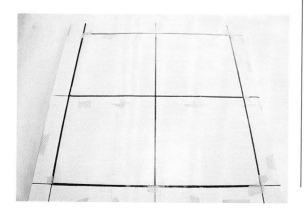

Applying the Glass Tiles

1. Arrange the glass tiles into a chessboard pattern.

> **Note:** These glass tiles were cut by Michael Johnston of Rainbow Vision Stained Glass. You can order them www.rainbowvisionsg.com or from your local glass company. Small porcelain or concrete tiles can be substituted for the glass.

2. Divide the glass tiles into equal quadrants.

When you place the tiles onto the contact paper, you will be working upside-down—the side that faces the paper will be the side that will show when the table is completed.

3. Place the first glass tile on the contact paper as shown. It should just touch the $\frac{1}{4}$-inch line but not overlap it. You'll want to keep $\frac{1}{4}$ inch space between each tile. Work from the center of the board out to the edges.

4. Add a second glass tile $\frac{1}{4}$ inch away from the first tile—in this case, each tile is $\frac{1}{4}$ inch thick, so another tile can be used as a spacer.

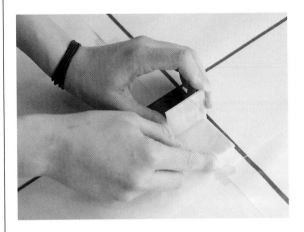

5. Continue placing tiles, working out from the center, to complete one quadrant of the game board.

Remember: Each tile should be separated from the others by ¼ inch. *And* the side you want to show on the finished table should be facing down.

6. Start on the next quadrant, working out from the center.

7. Continue placing the glass tiles onto the contact paper.

8. When the game board is complete, apply pressure to all of the tiles so they stick to the contact paper.

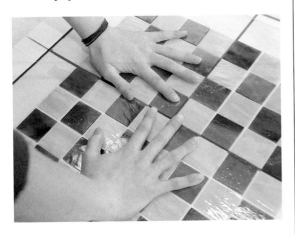

9. Next, make a frame for the tabletop mold. Cut two 20 x 2 x 1–inch boards and two 21¹⁄₂ x 2 x 1– boards.

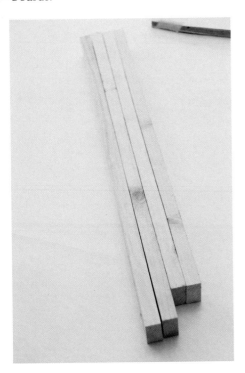

10. Build the mold by attaching the 21¹⁄₂ x 2 x 1–inch boards to the ends of the 20 x 2 x 1–inch board. Predrill, then screw the pieces together with 1¹⁄₄-inch drywall screws.

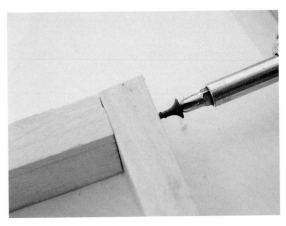

11. Predrill holes into the rails of the assembled table mold, three on each side.

12. Align the assembled table mold with the 20-inch square you drew on the paper.

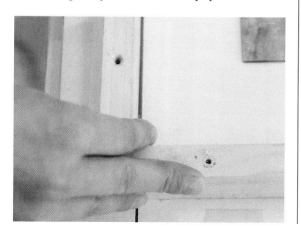

13. Screw the table mold into place on the plywood board with 2-inch drywall screws.

14. Prepare to build two mounting plates with the 1 x 2 x 22-inch boards and the 6 x 13-inch pieces of plywood.

15. Mark the centers of the 6 x 13-inch pieces of plywood.

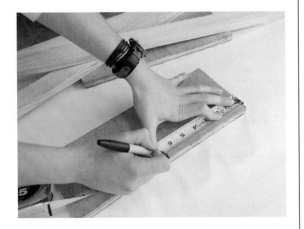

16. Mark the centers of the 22 x 1 x 2 boards.

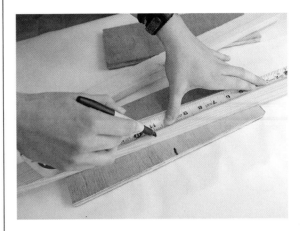

17. Screw the 22-inch board along the center of the plywood with 1¼-inch drywall screws.

18. Build the second mounting plate the same way. These plates will be embedded into the underside of the tabletop to allow a base to be attached.

19. Saturate the mounting plates with oil. You can also coat them heavily with resin as done in the circular tabletop project. The idea is to prevent the mounting plate from swelling with moisture, thereby cracking the cured concrete.

20. Mark the table mold at 6 inches from the edges.

21. Attach the mounting plates to the table mold at the 6-inch marks.

22. After the plates have been secured and you are comfortable with the construction of the mold, remove them to prepare for pouring the concrete. You will reuse the same screw holes after the cement is poured.

23. Cover the screw heads with tape.

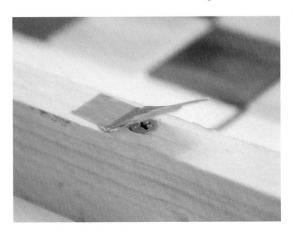

Filling the Mold

1. Mix concrete and pour some of it into the table mold. You will need about two-thirds of an 80-pound bag of premixed concrete to complete this project.

2. Push the concrete around the inside of the mold with a putty knife or a trowel, making sure that all the corners of the mold and the gaps between the glass tiles are filled. Be careful not to move the glass tiles.

3. Continue to fill the mold with concrete until it is about ¹/₂ inch from being completely filled.

4. Reattach the mounting plates.

5. Remove trapped air from the concrete by vibrating or tapping on the mold. Tapping lightly on all of the exposed wood will suffice. Don't vibrate or tap so vigorously as to loosen the glass squares from the contact paper.

6. Add more concrete.

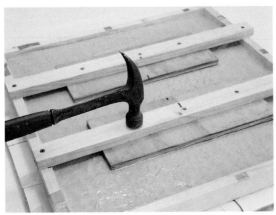

Don't forget to tap the tops of the mounting plates.

7. Tap or vibrate the mold until the concrete levels.

8. Continue adding small amounts of concrete and tapping it level until the mold is filled.

Light taps will usually suffice.

9. Don't overfill this mold—it is difficult to screed off the extra concrete with the mounting plate in the way.

10. Fill the mold to just the ends of the mounting plates, as shown.

11. Disassemble the mold after the concrete has cured.

Notice how easily this mold comes apart even when no mold release agent was used. That is because the concrete was poured onto a plastic surface. There is nothing for the concrete to grip onto, so no release agent was necessary.

Finishing the Table

1. Flip over the mold and pull it off the table-top.

2. Remove the contact paper from the table.

3. Look for "bug holes" on the table. These holes result from trapped air in the concrete and can be filled in if desired. Vibrating the mold during the pouring process will help release the trapped air. Some projects look more interesting with a lot of bug holes.

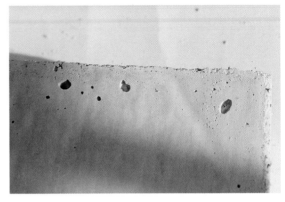

4. If you wish, fill in bug holes with a slurry of Portland cement and water.

5. Apply some of the slurry to the holes with a narrow putty knife and work the slurry into the holes.

6. Scrape off the excess slurry.

7. Look for bug holes between the glass tiles.

8. Apply the slurry and work it into all the holes, then scrape off the excess slurry.

9. Dampen a sponge in a bucket of water. Get as much water out of the sponge as you can. Too much water will pull the slurry out of the holes when you clean off the slurry residue.

10. Clean the slurry residue off with the damp sponge by working from the far side of the table to the close side. Rinse the sponge and repeat. Do not rub the sponge back and forth over the holes because it will pull out the slurry. Wipe in one direction and repeat while pulling all the excess slurry toward you.

The bug holes should look like this when they are filled.

11. Determine how you want the edges of the table to look.

One option is to use a brick rub on the edges. This will round the edges slightly. Brick rubs are available at hardware stores or home centers.

The rub creates a smooth, rounded edge.

Another option is to use a diamond grinder.

13. Clean off any excess concrete and Portland cement with water and a nylon scrub.

12. Finish the edges to your liking.

The surface of the tiles should be free of any stray concrete.

14. Decide if you like the color of the concrete.

15. Add color if desired.

16. Seal and/or wax the table. Apply a heavy coat to all sides of the table as well as the concrete between the tiles.

17. Mount the table to a base.

You can make a simple wood base, or repurpose an old table.

5. Stepping Stones

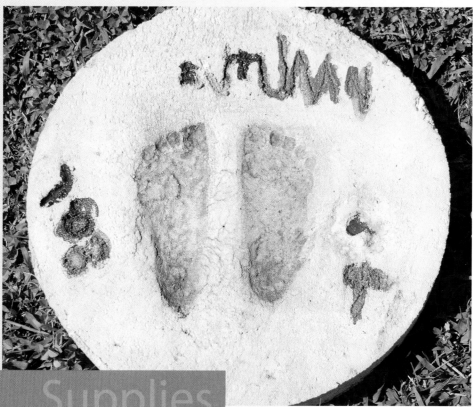

Supplies

- One 18-inch square of ³/₄-inch plywood
- One 72-inch strip of 2¹/₂-inch-wide hardboard
- 1¹/₄-inch drywall screws
- One 60-lb bag of premixed concrete
- One tube of acrylic caulk
- Fiberglass resin (optional)

Stepping stones can be used as fun accents in your garden or to make a pathway to your garden hose. Like all of the projects in this book, you can add your own flair. I asked my daughter to help with our stepping stone, which made for a fun afternoon.

1. Construct a mold at least 1 1/2 inches thick if the stone is to support the weight of human traffic. An 18-inch circular mold—constructed in the same way as the round tabletop mold—was used in this project.

2. Prepare enough concrete to fill your mold. We added green powdered color to this mix.

3. Apply a release agent, fill the mold, vibrate, and trowel the surface of the concrete as illustrated in previous projects.

4. Create a lasting memory by molding something precious to you into the surface of the stepping stone. We used my daughter's footprint. You could also use a pet's paw prints, a coin, a poem, or any number of precious mementos.

5. Press your child's foot into the concrete deep enough to make a visible impression.

6. Wash the foot thoroughly with water until there is no more slippery feeling. The slippery feeling is from the alkalinity (base) in the concrete, and it's best to rinse it all off.

Note: Do not allow your child to come in contact with concrete if your child has sensitive skin or you think they may have a bad reaction with concrete.

7. Allow your child to apply their finishing touches so they will forever be etched in stone.

8. After the concrete cures, your child can paint the stone to create a piece of art that will bring joy for years to come.

Making Stepping Stones with Fossil-like Imprints

1. Select a mold as described in the previous example and place a layer of interesting leaves in it.

2. Coat the leaves thoroughly with a mold release agent.

3. Place patties of concrete on top of the leaves.

4. Press the concrete onto the surfaces of the leaves only. Do not get concrete under the leaves.

5. Fill the mold to the rim and trowel it.

6. Allow the concrete to cure, then remove the stepping stone from the mold.

7. Pull all the leaves off the cured concrete.

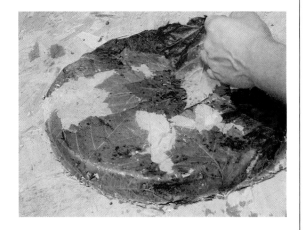

The leaves will leave interesting impressions of their veins, stems, and outlines.

> **Note:** Do not scrub off the leaves with a wire brush or anything hard because the leaf details can be destroyed.

8. Spray the concrete with a dark stain and let it soak in.

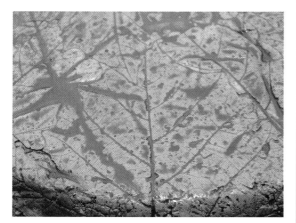

9. Sand the surface lightly.

10. Wash the surface of the stepping stone to reveal the detail from the leaves.

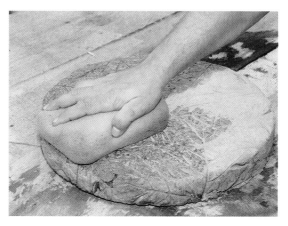

11. Allow the water to dry from the stepping stone, then seal it with a concrete sealer.

The finished stepping stone looks great in a garden or woodland setting.

6. Tapered Planter

Supplies

- One 4-foot x 8-foot x $5/8$-inch plywood board
- One 6-foot x 18-inch piece of corrugated cardboard
- $1\frac{1}{4}$-inch to $1\frac{5}{8}$-inch coarse drywall screws
- $1\frac{1}{2}$ x 8–inch PVC pipe
- Fiberglass resin (optional)
- Four 80-lb bags of concrete

This is the most difficult project in this book, but there's no reason to fear it. You just need to cut the board accurately when you are constructing the mold and follow the instructions carefully. The mold for this project will have two pieces: an outside mold and a center (inside) mold. The outside mold will contain the concrete, and the center mold will create the void that will be filled with soil. It's very important to wrap the center mold with cardboard as described so it can be easily removed from the concrete. If you make this planter with the lightweight concrete formula on page 7, allow it to cure in the mold for at least one week.

Constructing the Molds

1. Select a good quality ⅝-inch x 4-foot x 8-foot sheet of plywood and coat it thoroughly with fiberglass resin. Sand the resin in between coats.

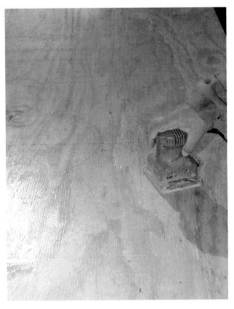

2. Cut the plywood to the dimensions specified on the diagrams. There will be a center mold and an outside mold. The outside mold will contain the concrete, and the center mold will create the void in the planter.

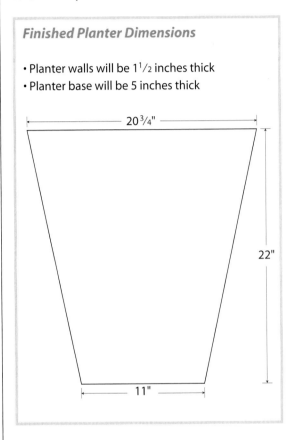

Finished Planter Dimensions

- Planter walls will be 1½ inches thick
- Planter base will be 5 inches thick

Outside Mold Pieces

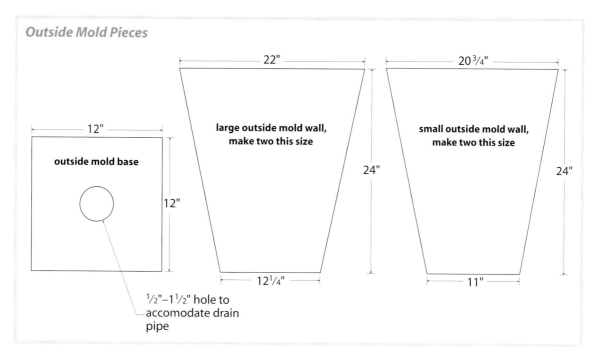

outside mold base

12"

12"

½"–1½" hole to accomodate drain pipe

large outside mold wall, make two this size

22"

24"

12¼"

small outside mold wall, make two this size

20¾"

24"

11"

Center Mold Pieces

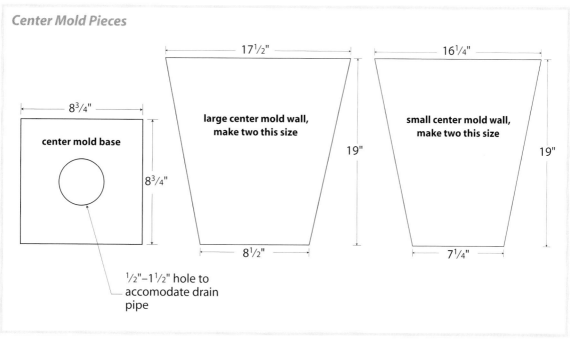

center mold base

8¾"

8¾"

½"–1½" hole to accomodate drain pipe

large center mold wall, make two this size

17½"

19"

8½"

small center mold wall, make two this size

16¼"

19"

7¼"

3. Mark the plywood accurately and cut out the first piece. This piece can be used as a pattern, so try to be extra careful to ensure accuracy.

4. Use the first piece you cut as a pattern and trace it. There will be eight sides and two bottoms to cut out. The inside mold and outside mold will be made from two pairs of plywood boards.

5. Continue cutting out the rest of the pieces, being careful to make accurate cuts. Don't cut too fast because it may cause the edges of the wood to splinter.

You should end up with eight pieces that look like this.

6. Identify the pieces by marking on the bare side of the wood.

7. Attach a large outside piece to the end of a small outside piece using drywall screws.

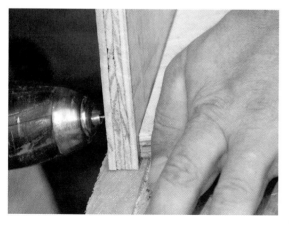

8. Continue attaching the other two pieces of the outside mold. Notice how the large outside piece screws into the side of the small outside piece.

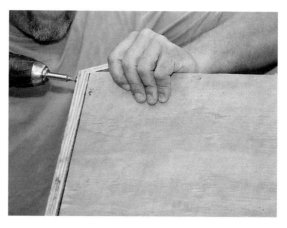

9. Assemble the center mold in the same manner. Again, the large pieces screw into the sides of the smaller pieces.

10. Cut four 2 x 4 x 12–inch pieces of wood to attach to the top inside of the center mold. These pieces will act as handles to pull the center mold out of the finished planter.

11. Attach the four two-by-fours to the top inside of the center mold.

12. Cut a piece of hardboard to cover the bottom of the center mold.

13. Attach the hardboard to the bottom of the center mold.

14. Sand off the overlapping ends of the hardboard and the corners of the center mold. Remember that the concrete will create the exact shape that it is poured into. It is important to eliminate any possibilities of the center mold getting stuck in the cured concrete.

15. Coat the outside of the center mold with fiberglass resin.

16. Cut and attach a square piece of plywood to fit on the bottom of the outside mold.

17. Drill a 1¹/₂ diameter hole into the exact center of the bottoms of both molds. These holes will hold the drainage pipe.

18. Attach two 2 x 4 x 12–inch boards at the center on the outside of the outside mold. Make sure these boards extend 1 inch above the top of the outside mold.

19. Attach a 34-inch board across the middle of the center mold. This will be used to secure the center mold once it is positioned properly in the outside mold and to later aid in removing the center mold from the cured concrete.

You are now finished with the woodworking part of this project and should have two molds that look like this. Notice how the center mold angles more than the outside mold. This will create more weight on the bottom of the planter, making it more stable. It will also make it easier to remove from the cured concrete.

Pouring the Concrete

1. Cover the outside surfaces of the center mold with corrugated cardboard. This is one of the most important steps. If the concrete adheres to the wooden surfaces of the center mold, it will be nearly impossible to remove it intact.

2. Simply trace the outside dimensions of the center mold onto the cardboard and cut it out.

3. Duct-tape the pieces of cardboard around the center mold. Cut the drain hole into the cardboard that covers the bottom of the mold.

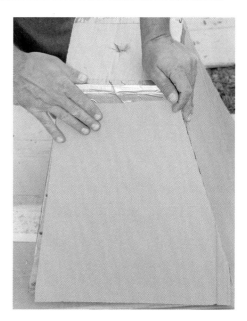

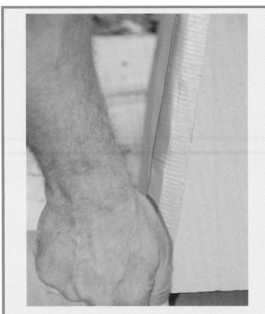

Note: You are making a cardboard sleeve around the mold. It should slip off of the mold easily, so tape the cardboard to the adjacent pieces of cardboard, not to the mold itself.

4. Put the center mold into the outside mold and insert a 7-inch-long pipe through both of the holes. I used 1-inch-inside-diameter PVC conduit, which has an outside diameter of about $1^3/_8$ inches.

5. Center the inside mold into the outside mold. You can use a piece of 2 x 4–inch lumber for a guide. Remember, a two-by-four is actually $1^1/_2$ x $3^1/_2$ inches. You should have a $1^1/_2$-inch space between the two molds at the top.

6. Secure the center mold to the outside mold after it is centered.

7. Cut one more piece of cardboard to cover the opening of the small mold and attach the cardboard with tape as shown. This will aid in pouring the concrete into the small openings.

A wetter concrete mix will work best for this project. You should use reinforcing fiber in this mix for extra strength and a water reducer to produce a more fluid concrete. If you are mixing in a wheelbarrow, however, use a high-strength pre-mixed bag.

8. Pour the concrete onto the cardboard and allow it to run into the openings of the assembled mold.

A piece of cardboard and a trowel will aid you in neatly filling the mold.

9. Vibrate the outside of the mold throughout the filling process.

10. After the mold is filled and vibrated, cover the planter and allow it to cure for at least two days at 70 degrees F, then remove it from the mold.

11. Remove the center first by tapping the center mold everywhere you can. *Do not hit it too hard or you may crack the planter.* The center mold will fit very tight, so be patient.

12. Remove any duct tape that may stop the center mold from being released.

Pull upwards firmly to release the center mold from the cardboard.

13. Remove the cardboard sleeve. Notice how the concrete mirrors the exact texture of the cardboard and duct tape.

14. Flip the planter upside down.

15. Remove the bottom of the mold, loosen a few screws, and the planter will drop out.

16. Remove the mold.

17. Push the pipe through the bottom of the planter until it's flush with the inside of the planter.

18. Saw off the pipe that extends past the bottom of the planter.

19. Flip the planter upright and rub off any rough edges with a brick rub.

20. Color and seal your planter to your liking.

Making a Hypertufa Planter

Tufa is a soft, porous rock that forms from dissolved calcium in bodies of water like springs and lakes. Historically, in Europe, tufa was the desired raw material to make livestock watering troughs because it was plentiful and easy to carve. Around the mid-1800s, collecting exotic plants became popular in England, and the tufa troughs provided an excellent home for the plants because of the porous nature of the tufa rock. Demand for tufa eventually outpaced the supply, making it very expensive. Enter hypertufa, which is simply a man-made version of the naturally formed calcite rock.

It's important to make hypertufa pots and troughs thicker than if made with standard concrete mix because hypertufa is not as strong. For small projects, make the walls about $1^{1}/_{2}$ inches thick. Make them thicker for larger projects.

1. To create a hypertufa planter, make a mold by selecting two containers that will form walls about 1½ inches thick. In this example, I used two old plant containers. Your local nursery may be willing to give away used containers. If you can't find used plant containers, cardboard boxes will also work.

2. Mix the lightweight formula found on page 7 in the same fashion as the other concrete recipes and pour it into the mold; it should be thick and claylike.

3. Allow the hypertufa to cure for about a week, then remove it from the mold.

4. Cut the outside mold to release the hardened pot.

5. Spray the pot with diluted muratic acid if you want the outside to look more worn.

6. As in previous projects, finish the pot with a color and shape to your liking.

7. Finally, drill a drainage hole in the bottom of the pot with a masonry drill.

7. Decorative Bowls

We are going to change the concrete mix for this project just to keep it interesting and help you create your own ideas. We will use recycled glass as an aggregate.

Making Concrete with a Glass Aggregate

1. Acquire scrap stained glass or colored glass bottles.

2. Put the glass into a bucket and cover it with water. The water will help keep glass chips and dust from flying out of the bucket when it is being smashed.

3. Smash the glass with a board. Wear gloves and protective eyeglasses for safety.

4. Continue smashing the glass until you create small nuggets of glass and glass sand.

Glass Aggregate Concrete Mix

Two parts glass aggregate
One part white Portland cement
One part sand
A pinch of fiber
Water

Mix the parts together in a bucket. A 16-ounce
cup is the unit of measurement for this mix.

Stir everything together until the mix reaches a
claylike consistency.

5. Another method of smashing the glass it to put it into a mixer with a few rocks and water and let the machine do the work.

6. Use the glass as an aggregate in a concrete mix.

Making the Bowls

You will need two bowls that will create a gap of about $5/8$ inch between them when they are stacked. Metal or plastic bowls will work best.

> **Note:** Use the cheapest metal or plastic bowls you can find. It's easier to remove the cured concrete from the mold if it flexes a little.

1. Coat the inside of the larger bowl with a release agent. It's extremely important to use a heavy coat of release agent with this project because, if it is not used, the concrete may never come out of the mold.

2. Thoroughly coat the outside of the smaller bowl with mold release.

3. Scoop some of the concrete mix into the larger bowl.

4. Work the concrete up onto the walls of the bowl using your trowel.

5. Push the smaller bowl into the concrete.

6. Keep the smaller bowl in place with a weight, such as a cinderblock. Make sure there is an even wall of concrete around the mold.

7. Scrape off the excess that oozes out with a putty knife or a trowel.

Using Woks to Make a Glass Aggregate Bowl

This is one of the simplest projects in the book and can be very versatile. Woks are handy for making use of small amounts of leftover concrete. They will create an interesting bowl if they are filled to the brim or will make a small dish if just a handful of concrete is used.

1. Coat the inside of the bottom wok and the outside of the top wok with a release agent.

> **Note:** The glass aggregate concrete recipe for this project will yield two bowls about 10 inches in diameter by $4^{1}/_{2}$ inches tall by $^{5}/_{8}$ inch thick. We made a second bowl from two woks to illustrate how to make another shaped bowl.

2. Scoop concrete into the wok and push it up onto the sides.

3. Push the top wok into the concrete.

4. Hold the woks together and bang them onto the working surface to evenly distribute the concrete and release air pockets.

> **Note:** Experiment to see how thin you can make the walls of the bowl. We've had success making the walls thinner than $1/2$ inch.

5. Set the wok mold into a bucket and weight it until it cures.

Removing the Cured Bowls from the Molds

1. The wok mold is the easiest to release. Because of its shape, the mold falls off the cured concrete.

2. The other mold needs a little more care. Tap the lip of the inside mold lightly.

3. Pry out the inside mold very carefully.

4. Tap the lip of the outside mold lightly onto the working surface. The concrete should slip out easily. Be very gentle removing the concrete because it is not fully cured and is still weak.

Finishing the Glass Aggregate Bowl

1. Sand or grind the surfaces to expose the glass.

The top rim will probably require some extra grinding.

2. Expose only the glass on the rim of a bowl if you prefer.

3. Grind a flat spot on the bottom of the bowl made from the wok molds if you want the bowl to sit flat on a surface. Because of the shape of the wok bowls, they rock back into an upright position when bumped, so you may decide to grind a flat bottom.

4. Verify if the bowl needs to be ground more or sanded more.

5. Finish the bowl to your liking.

Note: Notice how thin the rim is. It's important to use fiber mesh in this project for added strength. If the bowl cracks slightly, it won't fall apart because the mesh will hold it together.

Finishing the Concrete Bowls

You can apply color and texture after the concrete bowl cures for a few days. The finish is limited only by one's imagination. As you may have noticed, there isn't an exact step-by-step procedure for finishing the concrete in any of the projects in this book. The only suggestion is to wait until you are happy with the look before you seal and wax the bowl. Even if you do seal and wax the bowl, you can always sand the surfaces again and apply more stain until you are satisfied with the result.

You can smooth the rough edges of a bowl with a brick rub or leave them rough.

A diamond bit grinder wheel will make a machined edge.

Always wear protective eyeglasses, a dust mask, and work gloves when working with a grinder.

Drill a drain hole with a masonry bit if you are going to plant something in the bowl.

Apply a favorite color to a bowl.

At the far left is the edge of a lightweight bowl after it was machined with a diamond bit grinder. Notice the exposed perlite aggregate.

This photo shows exposed pea gravel aggregate after it was ground with a diamond bit.

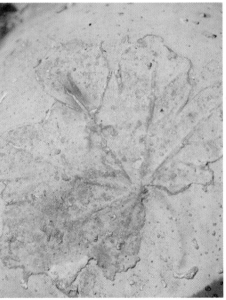

This bowl was molded with leaves placed between the smaller inside bowl and the concrete. Notice the fossil-like imprints. The glass aggregate is most visible along the rim.

Making Concrete Bowls in a Sand Mold

This is a fun project that you can make in your child's sandbox.

1. Soak a pile of sand with water.

2. Get a cheap mixing bowl made of thin steel or plastic.

3. Dig a hole in the wet sand large enough for the mixing bowl to fit into.

4. Place the bowl in the hole so it sits level.

5. Pack wet sand around the bowl.

6. Pack the sand hard so the bowl sits level with the sand. You are trying to create a mold that will hold concrete.

7. Carefully remove the bowl while making sure not to collapse the sand mold.

The sand mold should be as smooth as you can get it to be.

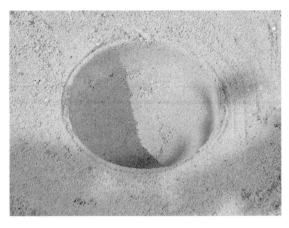

8. Take a handful of concrete and make a flat patty out of it.

> **Note:** The concrete used in this project was made with white Portland cement and blue powdered color.

9. Place several of these patties into the sand mold.

10. Set the bowl on top of the concrete and centered in the sand mold.

11. Push down hard on the rim of the bowl to force the concrete toward the sides of the sand mold. The sand mold will expand to accommodate the volume of concrete and the bowl.

12. Remove the bowl and check for holes and unevenness in the concrete.

13. Fill in any holes with more concrete.

14. Cover the bowl with a mold release.

15. Push the bowl back into the concrete.

16. Fill the bowl with sand to hold it in place.

17. Smooth around the edges of the bowl with a trowel or a flat paint scraper.

18. Allow the concrete to cure for a few days, then remove it from the sand.

19. Tap lightly around the rim of the bowl until it loosens from the concrete. Be careful not to hit the concrete.

20. Remove the bowl from the concrete.

21. Wash off the excess sand.

22. Use a grinding wheel or brick rub to grind the concrete bowl to the texture you prefer.

23. Inspect your new concrete bowl to determine if you like its finish.

24. Wash off any loose sand and dust.

25. Allow the concrete to dry, then apply a sealer inside and out.

The finished project has a rough-hewn appearance.

Making a Birdbath in a Sand Mold

Here's another fun project you can do in the sandbox. We made this birdbath using several leaves, but you could also use just one large leaf for your design.

1. Soak the sand with water.

2. Form a solid mound of sand by patting and smoothing the sand until it is about 6 inches tall and 24 inches in diameter.

3. Cover the sand mound with a piece of plastic.

4. Weigh the plastic down on its edges with sand.

5. Collect a group of large leaves.

6. Cut off the stems.

7. Arrange a few leaves on the plastic-covered sand mound and place a handful of concrete on top of them.

8. Place a few more leaves and concrete on the mound.

> **Note:** The consistency of the concrete should be thick and claylike for this project. This batch of concrete is the recommended recipe and has sand-colored dry dye mixed into it. Gray Portland cement was used.

9. Continue building with leaves and concrete to the edge of the mound.

10. Maintain a consistent thickness of concrete of about 1 inch over the entire mound.

11. Make impressions on the exposed concrete if you wish. The exposed concrete will be the underside of the birdbath.

12. Cover the concrete and allow it to cure for at least 24 hours. This project can be moved relatively soon after it was created because it does not have to be forcefully removed from a tight mold.

13. Wash off the concrete after you have determined that it is thoroughly cured.

14. Grind the rough edges with a brick rub.

15. Scrub off any embedded leaves with a plastic bristle brush.

16. Brush dark stain on the entire concave area of the birdbath.

17. Wipe off the excess stain to reveal the leaf details.

18. Reapply stain and wipe it off until you achieve a look you like.

19. Stain the underside in the same manner, then brush concrete sealer over the entire birdbath.

20. Place the finished birdbath on a stable base, fill with water, and enjoy.

Birds will appreciate the rough texture of the bath. It allows them to get a good grip. Place the birdbath near trees or shrubs so birds will have quick access to shelter. They won't use a bath that's too exposed. And don't forget to change the water frequently.

Concrete Craft Gallery

Here are a few examples of projects that were made using the techniques taught in this book. The possibilities are endless, and I hope that you are inspired to create your own vision.

Concrete pavers with black sand veins.

Detail of black sand veins.

Black sand used in veins. Black sand is actually anthracite coal, a very hard coal found in the Pennsylvania mountains.

These pavers were cast in coarse sand, giving them a rough texture.

These tables were molded as described in this book. After curing, they were marked, stained, and ground with a cutter wheel to accentuate the features.

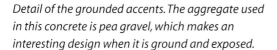

Detail of the grounded accents. The aggregate used in this concrete is pea gravel, which makes an interesting design when it is ground and exposed.

This is an example of a larger, differently shaped table. Concrete makes for great patio tables because it is impervious to weather and won't blow away.

This unique bathroom was made with custom concrete tiles. The tiles are stained gray concrete. The walls, made with a green powder color additive, are solid concrete poured on location.

This is another example of how to use the same techniques taught in this book to make another unique piece of furniture.

Leaves were rubber-cemented to the bottom of these tiles' molds prior to pouring the concrete. Powder color was also added to the mix to render the tiles' respective colors.

Tiles should keep their colors indefinitely as long as they are sealed properly. As mentioned earlier, if the color does fade or change, that's okay. Concrete will sometimes develop a patina with use over long periods of time.

These glass mosaic stepping stones were made using the same technique as the glass inlay chessboard.

Concrete bowls with various textures and colors.

This bowl was made with a two-wok mold using two different colors of concrete. Bent rebar handles were inserted into the wet concrete.

After the concrete cured, the edge of the bowl was ground and color stains were applied.

This bowl was sand-molded with a wok. The concrete mixture was 1/4 gray Portland cement and 3/4 white Portland cement with a yellow powder color additive and a pea-gravel aggregate. The vein was created by pouring a line of black sand into the sand mold prior to pouring the concrete.

A 36-inch bowl that was sand-molded from a wok. The handles and base were hand-molded into the sand.

Handle detail. A trowel was used to cut a crude design into the handle while the concrete was still wet.

An example of a handle ground out of a shallow bowl.

A practical use for a concrete bowl.

Planters can be made in a variety of shapes, depending on the mold.

These vases were made by cementing two bowl shapes together.

Detail of the cement holding the bowls together.

This concrete candleholder was made using a small rectangular mold.

The techniques taught in this book are the same techniques used to make this beautiful outdoor kitchen.

By now, if you are completely nuts about working with concrete, you may want to consider a project like this. The walls are precast slabs poured and stained off-site. The door is a precast slab with a geode molded into it to act as a handle. The countertop is a slab with exposed aggregate. And the sink is a solid molded chunk with a gentle slope to the drain.

Acknowledgments

Thank you from the deepest places in my soul to Stackpole Books and my friends and family for giving me the opportunity to create this book. An emotional and sincere thanks goes to my friend Ed McNamara, the man who worked through most of these projects with me and followed my demands, even when he was soaked with sweat and annoyed with my direction. He kept on going to finish the projects. To Mark Allison and Janelle Steen of Stackpole Books, who pushed me through, even though I was always late with their deadlines. Thanks to Mark, the "Sandalman" Dorward, who "infected" me with the desire to create things made of concrete. And to Jason Beigh, the man who introduced me to the idea that concrete is more than just a pavement. Thanks to my friend forever, Cindi Wycheck, for her assistance; my daughter, Autumn; and son, Josh. Also a special thanks to my niece Sarah Wycheck and nephew Joe Wycheck, who were always there if I needed an extra set of hands. And I thank Sun Precast, Pennsy Supply, J.C. Budding, Smith Stains, and Bondo brand for technical support and donations for this project.

Usage Formulas

Here are a few handy formulas that will help you determine how much concrete you'll need for your project. An 80-pound bag yields approximately 0.6 cubic feet of concrete.

Square or Rectangle
Volume = length X width X height

Cylinder
Volume = (*pi* X radius^2) X height
Pi is approximately 3.1416. The radius is half the diameter of the circle.

Pyramid
Volume = $^1/_3$ X base area X height
The base area is calculated by multiplying the length and width of the base.

Cone
Volume = ($^1/_3$ X *pi* X radius^2) X height
Pi is approximately 3.1416. The radius is half the diameter of the circle.

Resources

Budding Co.
www.buddingco.com
Sells concrete supplies.

Concrete Network
www.concretenetwork.com
Loaded with all things concrete. It is the best resource to find products in your area.

CSGNetwork
www.csgnetwork.com
Provides free calculations to determine volume and much more.

Online Conversion
www.onlineconversion.com
Provides good conversion calculators from metric to English.

Pacific Southwest Concrete Alliance
www.concreteresources.net
Provides many links and information mainly about architectural concrete.

Portland Cement Association
www.cement.org
This site provides interesting articles about concrete as well as technical data.

www.recycledbowls.com
Site of the author's current business in which we manufacture and sell bowls made of recycled materials.

Smith Stain Store
www.smithstainstore.com
A terrific concrete stain company that will give you more ideas on staining concrete.

The SO Factory
www.thinksofactory.com
Good source for additional ideas. It's owned by the author's former business partner, "Sandelman," who is also a distributer of Smith stains.

Cheng, Fu-Tung, *Concrete at Home.* Newtown, CT: The Taunton Press, 2005.

Hubar, Jean. *Decorative Concrete.* Menlo Park, CA: Sunset Publishing, 2007.

Hunter Warner, Sherri. *Creative Concrete Ornaments for the Garden.* New York, NY: Lark Books, 2005.